PROJECT
STEM
SCIENCE • TECHNOLOGY • ENGINEERING • MATHEMATICS

Building A Super Sneaker

Grades 3–5

Glenview, Illinois • Boston, Massachusetts • Chandler, Arizona • Upper Saddle River, New Jersey

LWAYS LEARNING

PEARSON

Teacher Reviewers

Candida M. Braun
West Fargo Public Schools
West Fargo, North Dakota

Sherri M. Gibson
Union Elementary STEM and
Demonstration School
Gallatin, Tennessee

Susan Holt
Union Elementary STEM and
Demonstration School
Gallatin, Tennessee

L. Jean Jackson
Old Mill Middle South
Annapolis, Maryland

Paul Keidel
Bismarck Public Schools
Bismarck, North Dakota

Martin Laine
Ayer-Shirley Middle School
Ayer, Massachusetts

Angelia Joy Long
Charles Carroll Middle School
New Carrollton, Maryland

Linda McShane
La Grange Public Schools District 102
La Grange Park, Illinois

Diana Mitchell
Union Elementary STEM and
Demonstration School
Gallatin, Tennessee

Bradd Smithson
John Glenn Middle School
Bedford, Massachusetts

Mary Reid Thompson
Union Elementary STEM and
Demonstration School
Gallatin, Tennessee

Leslie Yates
Union Elementary STEM and
Demonstration School
Gallatin, Tennessee

Acknowledgments

Photographs

Every effort has been made to secure permission and provide appropriate credit for photographic material. The publisher deeply regrets any omission and pledges to correct errors called to its attention in subsequent editions.

Unless otherwise acknowledged, all photographs are the property of Pearson Education, Inc.

Photo locators denoted as follows: Top (T), Center (C), Bottom (B), Left (L), Right (R), Background (Bkgd)

Building a Super Sneaker
Cover: (BL) ©Jamie Farrant/iStockphoto, (BL) ©Luminis/Shutterstock, (B) ©Otna Ydur/Shutterstock, (C) ©Pete Saloutos/Shutterstock, (L) ©Sadora/iStockphoto, (BL) ©Anatoly Vartanov/iStockphoto, (BC) ©Yaten Tau/Shutterstock; **ivS** (BC) Eckehard Schulz/©Associated Press; **vS** (CR) Car Culture/Corbis; **viS** ©Mariusz Blach/Fotolia; **viiS** (BR) ©Fernando Blanco Calzada/Shutterstock; **ixS** ©Philippe Pasaila/Photo Researchers, Inc.

Designing Bridges
Cover: (CR) ©advent/Shutterstock, (BL) ©Anatoly Vartanov/iStockphoto, (Bkgrd) ©Carlos E. Santa Maria/Shutterstock, (BR) ©Fernando Blanco Calzada/Shutterstock, ©Ice-Storm/Shutterstock; **ivB** (BC) Eckehard Schulz/©Associated Press; **vB** (CR) Car Culture/Corbis; **viB** ©Mariusz Blach/Fotolia; **viiB** (BR) ©Fernando Blanco Calzada/Shutterstock; **ixB** ©Andre Jenny/Alamy Images, ©Julie Quarry/Alamy Images; **xB** (CL) (CR) (BL) (BR)©Steve Speller/Alamy Images, Courtesy of Lockheed-Martin/U.S. Department of Defense.

PEARSON

ISBN-13: 978-0-13-319812-6
ISBN-10: 0-13-319812-X
3 4 5 6 7 8 9 10   VOUD   18 17 16 15 14

Project STEM

Introduction to STEM

Building a Super Sneaker

Appendices

Safety Symbols*

Making Measurements

Scientific Methods Flowchart

*Review the Safety Symbols pages before beginning each topic.

Building a Super Sneaker

The Engineering Design Process

Engineers are people who solve problems. They use the engineering design process described below to make new products. They may not follow these steps in the same order each time.

Identify a Need

When making a new product, engineers start by identifying a need or problem. Maybe a product is not working well. Maybe people need a new product. Engineers choose a problem or need to work on.

Research the Problem

Then, engineers gather information. They may find articles on the internet. They may find information in books and magazines. They may talk to other engineers. They might even conduct tests.

Design a Solution

Engineers use their research to find new solutions. Teams of engineers brainstorm ideas. During brainstorming, team members suggest design solutions. Often, one suggestion leads to other ideas.

As the team works, they take notes carefully. They write down all their ideas, sources, and material lists. They can use this information later if they need to. Or, others can use the notes to help them repeat the process.

Brainstorming usually results in many possible solutions. But engineers cannot build all these possible designs. They need to choose the best solution. To help them, they think about limits to their designs. Money and time are common limits.

Engineers also make trade-offs. In a trade-off, engineers trade one benefit of a design for another. For example, they might want to lower the cost of the product. To do this, they might use weaker materials. After making trade-offs and thinking about limits, engineers will choose the best solution.

ivS

Building a Super Sneaker

Build and Test a Prototype

Next, engineers build the solution they chose. This working model is called a prototype. Engineers test their prototype. They take measurements and collect data. Then they use the data to find out what works well. For example, they might try to find out if their solution is safe, sturdy, and easy to use.

Find Problems and Redesign

Engineers also test the model to find out what is not working well. They identify problems. They redesign the model to make it work better. Most designs need some changes before they are final.

Communicate the Solution

Engineers need to tell the people who build and use the product about the final design. They do this in different ways. They can make detailed drawings. They can write descriptions. They can organize their data in tables and graphs. Whatever they do, they must communicate their results in clear and precise ways.

What stage of the design process is this person completing?

vS

Building a Super Sneaker

What Is STEM?

At school, you probably have separate math classes, science classes, and English classes. But, can you use English in math class? Of course you can! You can use what you learn in one class to help you understand another. Applying what you learn is a big part of STEM: Science, Technology, Engineering and Math.

Science

Science is a way of learning about the world. Scientists observe nature.

They ask questions and conduct experiments to find out about nature.

They communicate their results to help us understand our world.

Technology

Technology is all around you.

It is not just computers and TVs.

Your pen, your pack, and even your shoes are examples of technology.

Technology is how people change the world to meet their needs.

STEM

Engineering

Engineering is using science to solve real-world problems.

Engineers find ways to meet our needs.

They apply scientific knowledge to build and improve technology.

You can use engineering to solve problems too.

Math

Math is a useful tool.

It can help you understand your data better. You can use charts and graphs to organize your data. You can use math to summarize your data.

People use math to solve problems in science, technology, and engineering.

Building a Super Sneaker

Look at your feet. What is on them? Athletic shoes. Sneakers. Running shoes. These are all names for those things on your feet.

The soles are the part of a shoe that touches the ground. A rubber company made the first shoes with rubber soles about a hundred years ago. They were called sneakers because they were so quiet.

Today, there are special shoes for different sports. They may help you run faster or jump higher. Athletic shoes are made to be light. They are made to help prevent injury. Some shoes can even tell you where you are!

Take It Further

Athletic shoes often have grooves on the bottom. These grooves keep you from slipping when you run. Make a drawing of the sole of your shoe. Include all of the grooves in the sole. Compare your drawing to the drawings of your classmates. How are they alike? How are they different?

Athletic shoes have been popular for a while. Doctors, athletes, and coaches have shared their ideas for the perfect shoe.

What Makes a Good Shoe?

Think about all the parts of your athletic shoes. Each part is designed with a purpose in mind. People who design athletic shoes do a lot of research. They watch athletes run and jump. They study how their bodies move. They study how their feet move.

Who designs athletic shoes? Believe it or not, engineers do! These engineers choose the materials for the shoes. They choose materials that will make the best shoe.

It is not just the look of the shoe that is important. Engineers want to make the shoes comfortable. They want shoes to help athletes perform more safely. They look for new materials to cushion and support the foot.

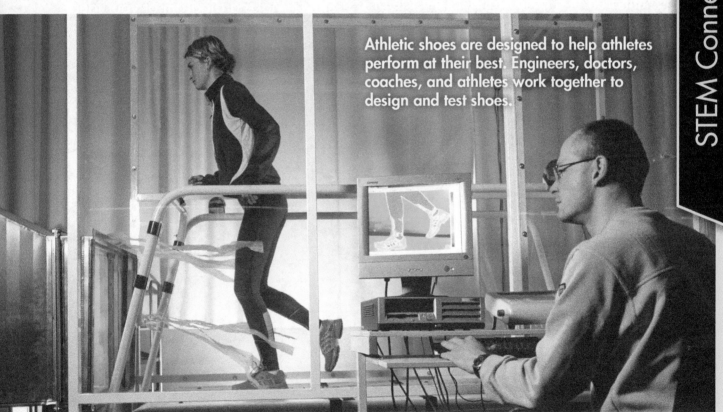

Athletic shoes are designed to help athletes perform at their best. Engineers, doctors, coaches, and athletes work together to design and test shoes.

Take It Further

Do you think you could design a better sneaker? What sport would it be for? What would it look like? Draw two pictures of the shoe you would design. Draw one picture that shows the shoe from the side. Draw a second picture that shows the sole of the shoe. Write a short description of your shoe. Describe the important features of your shoe. Include information that would make people want to buy your shoe.

Hi-Tech Kicks

GPS stands for Global Positioning System. A GPS uses satellites in space to track locations on Earth. Many people have a GPS in their cars. They can type in an address and get directions.

Some shoes have a GPS, too! Parents can buy shoes with a GPS in them to track their children. This safety feature allows parents to know where their kids are. Parents can even set limits for their children. If a child wanders outside of the limit, an alarm goes off.

The GPS can be used for athletes who are training. The GPS in the shoe maps where the runner is. It also tracks their pace. This helps runners know how fast they are running.

Take It Further

What would you like to see in your shoes? Think about the technology that you like to use on a daily basis. How would you put this technology into a shoe? Make a diagram of your ideal hi-tech shoe. Label each feature with a name and description.

This is a GPS satellite. It orbits the Earth. It receives signals from GPS units. It can track the units and send back information. The information tells the user their exact location on Earth.

Name _____ Date _____

Quick Lab Is It a Liquid or a Solid?

☑ **1.** Place some newspaper on your desk to work on.
Put 5 spoonfuls of cornstarch in a cup.
Add 3 spoonfuls of water.
Stir.

What is the ratio of cornstarch to water?

_____ to _____

☑ **2.** Pour the mixture into your hand. Does it have the properties of a liquid or a solid?

_____

☑ **3.** Close your hand and squeeze. How do the mixture's properties seem to change?

_____

Explain Your Results

4. Do you think your mixture is a liquid or a solid? Explain your reasons.

_____

_____

_____

Building a Super Sneaker

Vocabulary Practice

Use your textbook or a dictionary to help write a definition for each term.

Term	What it means
mixture	
property	
states of matter	
volume	the amount of space an object takes up
mass	
ratio	
materials	
polymer	

Building a Super Sneaker

Name _____ Date _____

Math Practice Understanding Ratios

Using ratios, you can compare the amounts of different things.

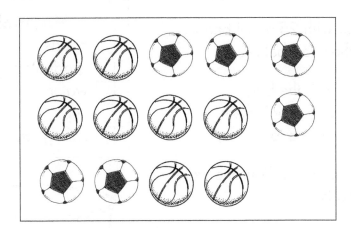

number of soccer balls: 6
number of basketballs: 8

The ratio of soccer balls to basketballs is

6   to   8.

1. What is the ratio of basketballs to the total number of balls?

_____ to _____

2. Simplify the ratio. Use common factors.

_____ to _____

Kari is making a mixture. She takes a bowl and adds the following ingredients:
10 spoonfuls of flour, 5 spoonfuls of sugar, and 1 spoonful of water.

3. What is the ratio of flour to sugar?

_____ to _____

Simplify. _____ to _____

4. What is the ratio of flour to the whole mixture?

_____ to _____

Building a Super Sneaker

Name _____ Date _____

Hands-on Inquiry
How Are Weight and Volume Affected When Objects Are Combined?

☑ **1.** Fill a graduated cylinder with 25 mL of beads. Record the volume on the chart below.

☑ **2.** Hold up the spring scale with the bag. Put the beads in the bag and weigh them. Record. Pour the beads into a cup.

☑ **3.** Repeat Steps 1 and 2 with water. Pour the water into the cup with the beads.

☑ **4.** Repeat Steps 1 and 2 with the mixture.

Materials
☐ beads
☐ graduated cylinder
☐ water
☐ cup
☐ spring scale with bag

Measurements of Matter		
	Volume (mL)	**Weight** (g)
beads		
water		
beads and water		

Explain Your Results

5. Did the total volume or weight change after mixing? Explain.

_____

_____

6. What is the ratio of beads to beads and water? Water to beads and water?

_____

Building a Super Sneaker

Faster! Higher! Farther!

Think about your athletic shoes. Do they help you run fast, stop quickly, or jump high? A shoe's comfort, support, grip, bounce, and flexibility depend a lot on the shoe's sole. As a volunteer footwear designer for your school's basketball team, you must make and experiment with a new material for the sole of a shoe.

Identify the Problem

☑ **1.** What problem will your shoe material help solve? _____

_____

_____

Do Research

Examine your classmates' shoes.

☑ **2.** What materials are the soles of these shoes made of? _____

_____

☑ **3.** What does each of these materials do for the shoe? _____

_____

_____

Go to the materials station(s) and make two mixtures in two separate bowls:

Mixture A	Mixture B
Mix 240 mL water and 15 mL borax.	Mix 120 mL water and 60 mL glue.

☑ **4.** Put 60 mL of Mixture A and 60 mL of Mixture B in a resealable bag. Seal the bag and knead the mixtures together with your hands. Tell what happens.

_____

_____

5S

Building a Super Sneaker

Name _____ Date _____

Store the mixture in the bag until later.

☑ **5.** Choose and describe a specific purpose of the shoes you are designing. _____

_____

_____

☑ **6.** How could you change the mixture in the bag (using only water, glue, and borax) to be more useful as sole material for the shoes you are designing? _____

_____

_____

☑ **7.** What are your design constraints? _____

_____

_____

Develop Possible Solutions

☑ **8.** Describe two different ways you could change the recipe that might solve the problem you identified. _____

_____

_____

Choose One Solution

☑ **9.** Describe how you will change the recipe and state your desired outcome. _____

_____

_____

_____

Building a Super Sneaker

☑**10.** List any additional materials you will need. _____

_____

_____

_____

Design and Construct a Prototype

☑**11.** Gather the materials you need, including any measuring cups or measuring spoons. Starting from scratch, make your new shoe material. As you make the material, measure and record how much of each ingredient you add.

Water: _____

Glue: _____

Borax: _____

Write the ratio of water to glue to borax you used in your design.

_____ to _____ to _____

Test the Prototype

Test your material by observing the changes caused by adding ingredients.

☑**12.** Describe how the new materials compare with the material made with your original recipe.

_____

_____

_____

_____

_____

Name _____   Date _____

Communicate Results

☑ **13.** Describe your results. Tell how well your material solved the problem you were trying to solve. Share your results with your classmates. _____

_____

_____

_____

_____

Evaluate and Redesign

☑ **14.** What changes could you make to the recipe to make your material better? Tell exactly how you will redesign your recipe.

_____

_____

_____

_____

☑ **15.** Mix up your revised recipe and test it. How well did it work? Explain.

_____

_____

_____

_____

Building a Super Sneaker

Career Spotlight Materials Engineer

When you design something, you have to choose the right materials. An earthquake-proof building, a fire-resistant rocket ship, and even a hiking shoe will only work well if they are made from the right materials. Sometimes a new material needs to be developed. This is what materials engineers do.

They learn all about different kinds of materials. They study the strength and other properties of materials. They test materials. Sometimes they develop new materials for a special purpose.

Materials engineers sometimes work with polymers. Polymers are materials made from long chains of molecules. Some polymers, such as cellulose and natural rubber, come from nature. Other polymers, such as plastics and nylon, are artificially made.

People who design sneakers might work with both materials engineers and biomechanical engineers. Biomechanical engineers study how shoes work with feet when playing sports. They figure out what a sneaker should be like to help athletes in a particular sport. Materials engineers figure out how to make that sneaker.

For example, a biomechanical engineer may suggest making running shoes with a flexible and springy sole. A materials engineer will figure out what kind of polymer will make a springier sneaker. In other cases, materials engineers might figure out how to make a shoe with cleats that will dig into the ground, or a sneaker that weighs less and lets more air in.

Building a Super Sneaker

Name _____   Date _____

Check Your Understanding

1. How are biomechanical engineers and materials engineers the same? How are they different?

_____

_____

_____

2. What other kinds of engineers might a materials engineer work with? Explain.

_____

_____

_____

3. You are a materials engineer. The company you work for is making picnic tables. You have two types of wood to choose from to make the tabletops.

One type of wood is thin, durable, and flexible. The other type of wood is thick, wears out easily, and is stiff. Tell which type of wood you would use and explain why you made your choice.

_____

_____

_____

_____

Building a Super Sneaker

Technology Zone Sneaker Features

Which sneaker is best? It depends on two things: what sport you play and shoe technology.

Most sneakers are **specialized,** or designed especially for a particular sport. Wrestling shoes are designed to be light and flexible. Soccer shoes have cleats, or bumps on the bottom of the sole. These cleats grip the ground. Basketball shoes are made for jumping. They are also made for changing direction quickly on a smooth surface.

Shoe designers also develop new technologies. They try to make better shoes all the time. They may want to make shoes that have more cushion. They may want to make shoes that are lighter or stronger.

Some sneakers have gas-filled pockets in their soles. These help cushion feet as people run. Some have tops made with a thin, strong mesh that is light and flexible and keeps your feet cool. Some have soles shaped in new and different ways.

All of this can make it hard to settle on a pair when you go sneaker shopping. On the other hand, it means that whatever you do, there is a perfect sneaker for you.

Building a Super Sneaker

Check Your Understanding

1. What do you think the first sneakers were made of?

_____

2. What features do you think a running shoe should have? Explain your answer.

_____

_____

_____

3. Choose a sport that you like. Draw a shoe that you think would be good for that sport. Label at least three features in your drawing. Write a sentence about why you think each feature is important for that sport.

Sport: _____

Building a Super Sneaker

Enrichment What Is a Polymer?

The material you made in the Quick Lab was not a polymer. It was a liquid with cornstarch suspended, or floating evenly, in the water. In the STEM Project, you experimented with polymers. A polymer is a group of smaller molecules all joined together to form a larger molecule. Think of it as a brick wall. The smaller molecules are the individual bricks. The polymer is the wall. In the wall, cement holds the bricks together. In the polymer, chemical bonds hold the smaller molecules together.

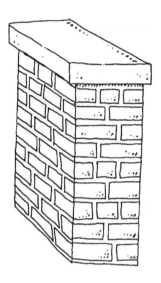

In a polymer, one type of molecule is strung together like a chain. Because of this, they can have different properties from the original material.

1. How was your water and cornstarch like a polymer?

_____

_____

2. How was your water and cornstarch different from a polymer?

_____

3. How can using polymers in a shoe design improve the shoe?

_____

_____

Building a Super Sneaker

Name _____ Date _____

Assessment Building a Super Sneaker

Circle the best answer to complete the sentence.

1. A _____ is used to compare a mass that you know with one that you don't know. (pan balance, graduated cylinder)

2. A material that can stretch and feels like rubber is likely to be a _____. (liquid, polymer)

3. Volume is the amount of _____ that something takes up. (matter, space)

4. Jimi is making a polymer. He adds 30 milliliters of borax solution and 20 milliliters of glue.

What is the ratio of borax solution to glue?

_____ to _____

5. Simplify the ratio.

_____ to _____

? How can you make a better sole for a athletic shoe?

6. Name two materials you would use in a sneaker. Tell how and why you would use the two materials.

_____

_____

_____

_____

_____

Name _____ Date _____

Look at the picture below.

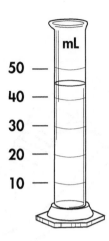

7. What is the volume of liquid?

   a. 40 mL

   b. 45 mL

   c. 55 mL

   d. You cannot tell from the picture.

8. What is the mass of the liquid?

   a. 40 g

   b. 45 g

   c. 55 g

   d. You cannot tell from the picture.

9. A student finds a small, unknown object during a recent scientific dig. Explain how the student can find the mass of the object. Include in your answer the units the student should use to record the mass.

_____

_____

_____

Building a Super Sneaker

Performance Assessment
A Composite Shoe Sole

The sole of a shoe can be made of different materials used together. An object that is made of different materials used together is called a **composite.**

Many shoe soles are composites. For example, a shoe sole might use foam in the center to absorb more shock. It might have rubber on the outside to hold everything together and to make the shoe last longer.

A shoe manufacturer wants to know how you would use your polymer to make a complete shoe sole. Your task is to integrate your polymer into the design of a shoe sole.

Design It

1. **Design** How will you integrate your polymer into a shoe sole? Draw a picture and label the different parts.

Building a Super Sneaker

Standardized Test Prep

Circle the letter of the best answer.

1. Which of these statements is **not** true about polymers?

A Some come from nature, and some are artificially made.

B They are large molecules formed by many smaller molecules bonded together.

C They are mixtures of smaller molecules suspended in a solvent.

D Their properties can be changed by varying the ratio of materials used to make them.

2. A materials engineer develops a new polymer made with 4 grams A and 6 grams B. Which choice gives the recipe as a simplified ratio of A to B?

A 4 to 6

B 6 to 4

C 3 to 2

D 2 to 3

3. A company wants to make a more comfortable chair. Which of the following tasks should **not** be included in the research stage of the engineering design process?

A Gather all the materials needed to construct a prototype.

B Consider the materials that can be used to make the chair.

C Ask a group of people what they like and dislike about their chairs.

D Begin designing a prototype of the chair.

Building a Super Sneaker

Lab Safety

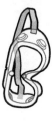

Always follow these rules to stay safe in the science lab.

- Read the activity carefully before you start.
- Listen to the teacher's instructions. Ask questions about things you do not understand.
- Keep you work area neat and clean. Clean up spills right away.
- Never taste or smell any substance unless directed to do so by your teacher.
- Handle sharp items and other equipment carefully.
- Use chemicals carefully. Dispose of chemicals properly.
- Help keep plants and animals that you use safe.
- Tell your teacher if there is an accident or if you see anything that looks unsafe.
- Wash your hands when you are finished.
- Wear safety goggles and gloves when necessary.
- Tie back long hair.

Look for this stop sign in your book. It warns you that you need to be careful. Follow the directions after the sign to stay safe in the lab.

Laboratory Safety Contract

I, _____,
(print full name)

have read the Laboratory Safety Rules. I understand their contents completely. I agree to follow all safety rules and guidelines for each of the following categories:

(please check)

☑ Wear safety equipment when necessary.

☑ Listen to the teacher.

☑ Report accidents immediately.

☑ Handle tools carefully.

☑ Keep my workplace clean.

☑ Clean up spills.

☑ Wash my hands after an activity.

☑ Use chemicals carefully.

☑ Keep plants and animals safe.

_____
(signature)

Date _____

Making Measurements

Scientists use measurements to record precise observations. They also use measurements to communicate their findings.

Measuring in SI

Scientists use the **International System of Units (SI)** as their standard system of measurement. SI units are easy to use. Each unit is ten times greater than the next smallest unit. The table lists some SI prefixes. These prefixes name the most common SI units.

Common SI Prefixes

Prefix	Symbol	Meaning
kilo-	k	1,000
hecto-	h	100
deca-	da	10
deci-	d	0.1 (one tenth)
centi-	c	0.01 (one hundredth)
milli-	m	0.001 (one thousandth)

Mass

Mass is measured in **grams (g)**. Mass is the amount of matter in an object. One gram is about the mass of a paper clip. Larger masses are measured in kilograms (kg). Scientists use a balance to find the mass of an object.

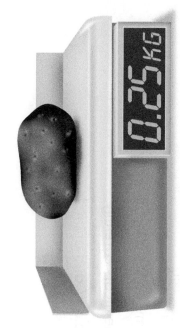

Common Conversion

1 kg = 1,000 g

The mass of the potato is 0.25 kg or 250 g.

Temperature

Scientists use the **Celsius scale** to measure temperature. Temperature is recorded in degrees Celsius (°C). Water freezes at 0°C and boils at 100°C. Scientists measure temperature using a thermometer.

The temperature of the water is 35°C.

Length

Length is measured in **meters (m)**. Length is the distance between two points. The distance from the floor to a doorknob is about one meter. Long distances are measured in kilometers (km). Short distances are measured in centimeters (cm) or millimeters (mm). Scientists use metric rulers and meter sticks to measure length.

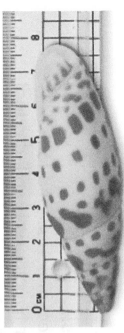
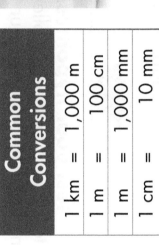

This shell is 7.8 cm or 78 mm.

Common Conversions

1 km	=	1,000 m
1 m	=	100 cm
1 m	=	1,000 mm
1 cm	=	10 mm

Liquid Volume

Liquid volume is measured in **liters (L)**. Liquid volume is the amount of space a liquid takes up. One liter is about the volume of a medium-size milk container. Smaller volumes are measured in milliliters (mL). Scientists use graduated cylinders to measure liquid volume.

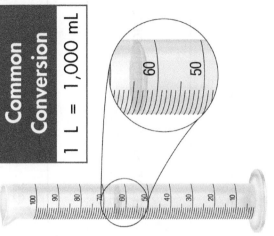

The volume of water in the graduated cylinder is 62 mL.

Common Conversion

1 L	=	1,000 mL

Time

Scientists measure time in **seconds (s)**. Time is how long something takes. There are 60 seconds in one minute. Longer times are measured in hours or days. Scientists use stopwatches and timers to measure time.

Common Conversions

1 hour	=	60 minutes
1 minute	=	60 seconds

Scientific Methods

Scientific methods are organized ways to answer questions and solve problems. Scientific methods help scientists draw conclusions. Scientists do not always use the same methods.

Ask a question.

Ask a question that you want answered. You might have a question about something you observe.

State your hypothesis.

A hypothesis is a possible answer to your question. It often predicts an outcome of an experiment. Write it as an *If...then...because* statement.

Identify and Control Variables.

Variables are things that can change. For a fair test, choose just one variable to change. Keep the other variables the same.

Test your hypothesis.

Make a plan to test your hypothesis. Collect materials and tools. Then follow your plan. Each time you test your hypothesis is called a trial. Repeat each trial three times.

Collect and record your data.

Keep good records of what you do and find out.
Use tables and pictures to help.

Interpret your data.

Organize your notes and records to make them clear.
Make diagrams, charts, or graphs to help.

State your conclusion.

Your conclusion is a decision you make based on your data.
Communicate what you found out. Tell whether your data supported your hypothesis.

Try it again.

Do the experiment a few more times.
The results of one experiment might not be right.
Be sure to do everything exactly the same each time.

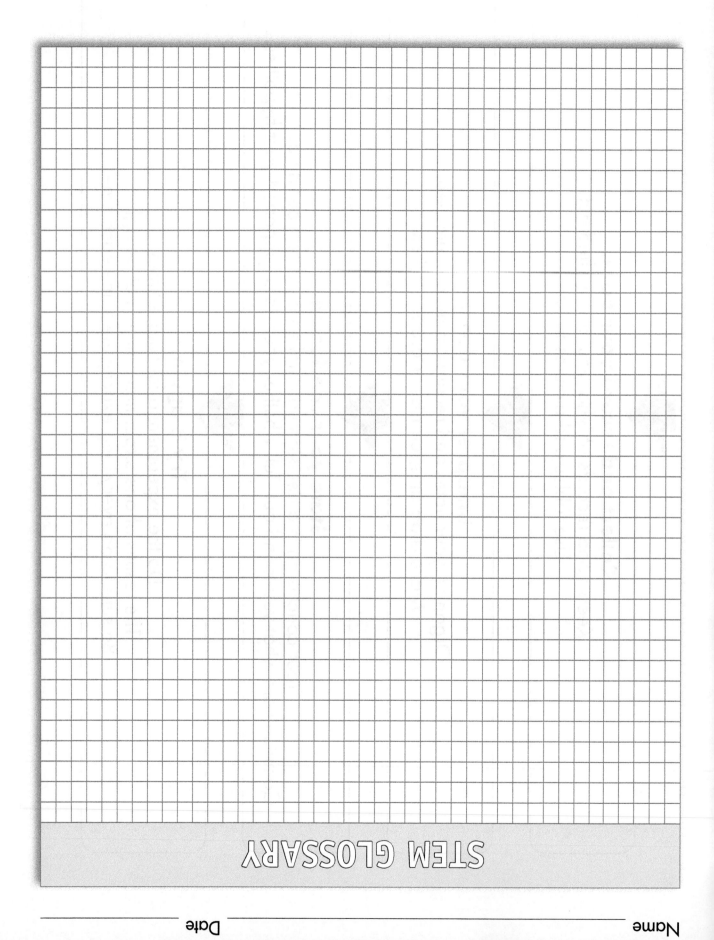

STEM GLOSSARY

STEM GLOSSARY

Designing Bridges

Grades 3–5

Glenview, Illinois • Boston, Massachusetts • Chandler, Arizona • Upper Saddle River, New Jersey

ALWAYS LEARNING

PEARSON

Designing Bridges

Grades 3–5

Glenview, Illinois • Boston, Massachusetts • Chandler, Arizona • Upper Saddle River, New Jersey

Project STEM

Introduction to STEM

Designing Bridges

Appendices

Scientific Methods Flowchart

Making Measurements

Safety Symbols*

Review the Safety Symbols pages before beginning each topic.

The Engineering Design Process

Engineers are people who solve problems. They use the engineering design process described below to make new products. They may not follow these steps in the same order each time.

Identify a Need

When making a new product, engineers start by identifying a need or problem. Maybe a product is not working well. Maybe people need a new product. Engineers choose a problem or need to work on.

Research the Problem

Then, engineers gather information. They may find articles on the internet. They may find information in books and magazines. They may talk to other engineers. They might even conduct tests.

Design a Solution

Engineers use their research to find new solutions. Teams of engineers brainstorm ideas. During brainstorming, team members suggest design solutions. Often, one suggestion leads to other ideas.

As the team works, they take notes carefully. They write down all their ideas, sources, and material lists. They can use this information later if they need to. Or, others can use the notes to help them repeat the process.

Brainstorming usually results in many possible solutions. But engineers cannot build all these possible designs. They need to choose the best solution. To help them, they think about limits to their designs. Money and time are common limits.

Engineers also make trade-offs. In a trade-off, engineers trade one benefit of a design for another. For example, they might want to lower the cost of the product. To do this, they might use weaker materials. After making trade-offs and thinking about limits, engineers will choose the best solution.

Build and Test a Prototype

Next, engineers build the solution they chose. This working model is called a prototype. Engineers test their prototype. They take measurements and collect data. Then they use the data to find out what works well. For example, they might try to find out if their solution is safe, sturdy, and easy to use.

Find Problems and Redesign

Engineers also test the model to find out what is not working well. They identify problems. They redesign the model to make it work better. Most designs need some changes before they are final.

Communicate the Solution

Engineers need to tell the people who build and use the product about the final design. They do this in different ways. They can make detailed drawings. They can write descriptions. They can organize their data in tables and graphs. Whatever they do, they must communicate their results in clear and precise ways.

What stage of the design process is this person completing?

vB
Designing Bridges

What Is STEM?

At school, you probably have separate math classes, science classes, and English classes. But, can you use English in math class? Of course you can! You can use what you learn in one class to help you understand another. Applying what you learn is a big part of STEM: Science, Technology, Engineering and Math.

Science

Science is a way of learning about the world. Scientists observe nature.

They ask questions and conduct experiments to find out about nature.

They communicate their results to help us understand our world.

Technology

Technology is all around you.

It is not just computers and TVs.

Your pen, your pack, and even your shoes are examples of technology.

Technology is how people change the world to meet their needs.

STEM

Engineering

Engineering is using science to solve real-world problems.

Engineers find ways to meet our needs.

They apply scientific knowledge to build and improve technology.

You can use engineering to solve problems too.

Math

Math is a useful tool.

It can help you understand your data better. You can use charts and graphs to organize your data. You can use math to summarize your data.

People use math to solve problems in science, technology, and engineering.

BRIDGES

The Skywalk is a glass-bottom bridge that extends over the Grand Canyon. It is suspended over 4,000 feet above the floor of the canyon. It extends out 70 feet from the edge of the canyon.

You want to cross a stream without getting wet. You lay a piece of wood across the stream and walk on the wood. Congratulations! You built a bridge!

A bridge can be simple. A log that is laid across water is a bridge. A bridge can also be complicated. Many bridges that cars drive across are made of steel beams and wires.

All bridges have one thing in common. They must have a balance of tension (stretching) and compression (squeezing) to be stable. Bridge builders have to make sure a bridge is stable. They need to know what distance the bridge must cover. They also need to know the materials they can use. This information helps the builder design a safe bridge.

Take It Further

There are many different types of bridges. Visit "Building Big: Bridges" at the PBS website. Look at "Bridge Basics" to learn about bridge types. Read about the different ways bridges can be built. What types of bridges are in your community?

The Liberty Bridge in Greenville, South Carolina was designed to look like it is floating on air.

Bridging the Gap Between Art and Science

Bridges are often designed and built by civil engineers. Civil engineers must make sure that the bridge does not cost too much. They must also make sure that the bridge is stable and that it does not fall apart in bad weather.

Lately, architects are also helping to design bridges. Architects use their creativity to make bridges stand out. Many of the bridges today are works of art. The next time you are crossing a bridge, think about the civil engineer who made the bridge safe and the architect who made it look beautiful.

Take It Further

When civil engineers and architects design a bridge, they must think about every detail. The engineer might make sure the bridge can hold a certain amount of weight. The architect might make sure that the bridge fits in with the landscape around it. Does the bridge need lights, signs, or other accessories? Suppose you are asked to design a bridge. What questions would you need answered before you begin your design?

Designed to Move

Think about words that you could use to describe bridges: strong, rigid, stable. How about movable?

Some bridges are made to move, so that boats or ships may pass beneath them. Movable bridges can move in different ways. Some lift like an elevator, and some swing to the side. Others work like a drawbridge on a medieval castle. One bridge in London, England rolls up like a pill bug.

There are different ways that these bridges move. Some use hydraulics, and others use gears and motors.

Take It Further

Is there a movable bridge in your community? If so, find out how it works. Does it lift up? Does it swing to the side? Does it use hydraulics or gears and motors? If your community does not have a movable bridge, find one on the Internet and read about it.

The Rolling Bridge in London, England rolls up to allow boats to pass.

Name _____ Date _____

Quick Lab How Does Tube Shape Affect Strength?

The shape and design of a tube affects the strength of the tube.

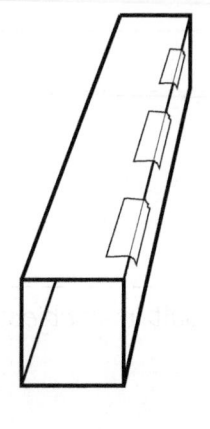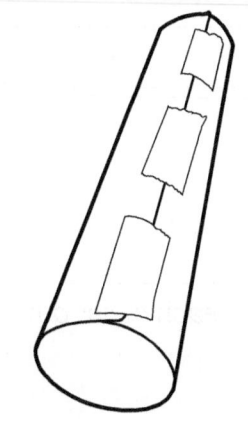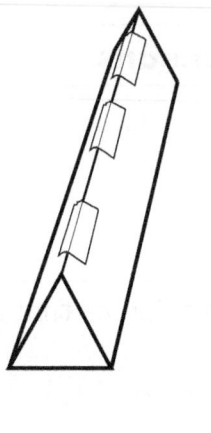

Materials
- [ ] strong paper
- [ ] tape
- [ ] books

☑ **1.** Choose a shape and design of your tube. Make three tubes of the same shape using the paper and tape.

☑ **2.** Set a tube upright. Test it by adding books one at a time until it collapses.

☑ **3.** Record the number of books the tube held up in the table below.

☑ **4.** Repeat Steps 2 and 3 with your other two tubes.

Tube Testing Results	
Tube Number	**Number of Books**
1	
2	
3	

Explain Your Results

5. Did each of your tubes collapse under the same amount of weight? What in the design contributed to the collapse? Explain your reasoning.

_____

_____

Vocabulary Practice

Use your textbook or a dictionary to help write a definition for each term.

Term	What it means
centimeter	
balanced forces	a collection of forces that balance each other out and result in an object not moving
decimeter	
force	
structural engineer	
suspension bridge	
truss	

Designing Bridges

Math Practice Using Centimeters and Decimeters

A centimeter (cm) is a unit of length that is used to measure small objects.
A decimeter (dm) is 10 cm long.

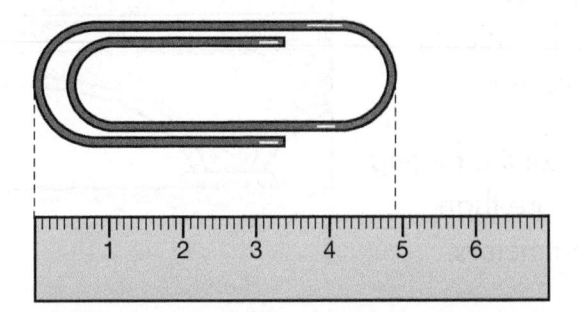

1. How long is the paper clip in centimeters? _____ cm

2. How long would two paper clips be in centimeters? _____ cm

3. How long would two paper clips be in decimeters? _____ dm

---

4. Measure the length of the pencil below to the nearest centimeter.

_____

5. Measure the height of the cup below to the nearest centimeter. Then measure the width at the cup mouth to the nearest centimeter.

height _____

width _____

Name _____ Date _____

Hands-on Inquiry Building a Strong Footing

One of the design constraints for bridges is the space available to place the footing for the bridge. You will design and test a footing by adding books until the footing collapses.

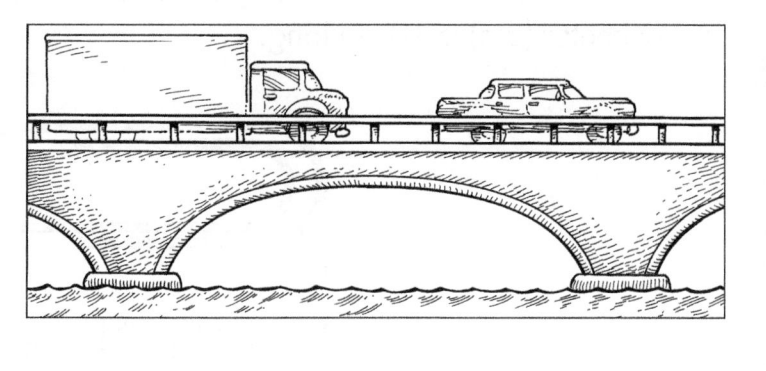

Your design constraint is that the footing must fit into an area no more than 10 centimeters by 10 centimeters.

☑ **1.** Design your footing. Make a drawing. Use the drawing when you build your footing design.

☑ **2.** Set the footing design in the testing area. Test the footing design by adding books one at a time until any part of the footing collapses. Wait 10 seconds before adding another book.

☑ **3.** Record the number of books the footing held up. Do not count the book that caused the tube to collapse. _____

Explain Your Results

4. When the footing collapsed, how did it collapse?

_____

_____

5. Identify a strength and a weakness in the footing.

_____

_____

_____

Technology Zone Suspension Bridges

Although bridges have been around for centuries, advances in technology
have made them stronger and more stable. A more modern version of a bridge is
the suspension bridge. A suspension bridge hangs a deck on ropes or cables. The deck
is for a road or a foot path. Suspension bridges are often built across busy waterways
because they are light and strong.

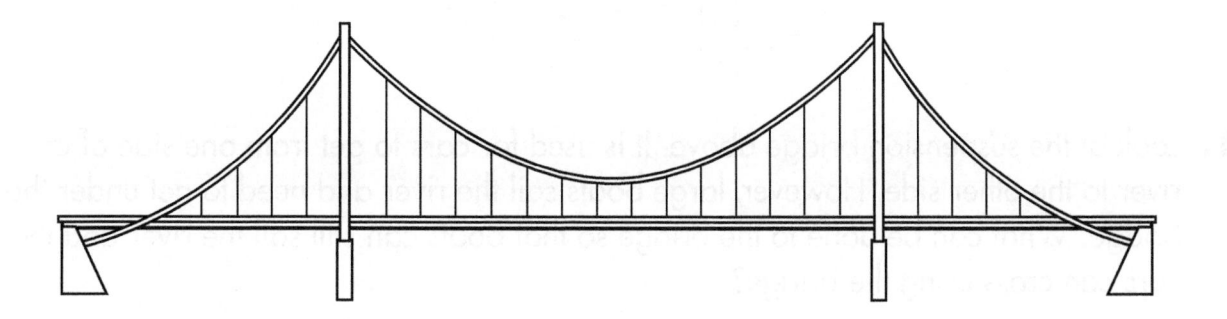

Years ago, simple suspension bridges were made from rope and wood. Modern
suspension bridges use box-section roadway supported by high-tensile-strength cables.
The cables are made of thousands of individual steel wires woven tightly. If one of the wires
breaks, there are still many others that will keep the bridge suspended.

Designing Bridges

Check Your Understanding

1. Look at the suspension bridge above. It is used for cars to get from one side of a river to the other side. However, large boats sail the river and need to get under the bridge. What can be done to the bridge so that boats can still sail the river and the cars can cross using the bridge?

_____

_____

_____

2. The earthquake in San Francisco in 1989 caused a lot of damage to the city's bridges. What features would you include in your design to make the bridge withstand earthquakes?

_____

_____

_____

_____

_____

_____

_____

Designing Bridges

Bridge the Gap

Bridges serve an important purpose. They allow people to pass over canyons, bodies of water, roads, and other obstacles that are difficult to cross. Bridges have many designs. As part of a team designing a model railroad, design a bridge that can span a distance of 40 centimeters.

Identify the Problem

☑ **1.** What problem will your bridge help solve? _____

_____

☑ **2.** What need will your bridge fulfill? _____

_____

Do Research

Examine pictures of different bridges. Describe the support system of the three different types of bridges.

☑ **3.** Beam bridge: _____

_____

☑ **4.** Arch bridge: _____

_____

☑ **5.** Suspension bridge: _____

_____

Go to the materials station(s). Pick up each item one at a time. Think about how it may or may not be useful in your design. Leave the materials where they are.

☑ **6.** What are your design constraints? _____

_____

Designing Bridges

Develop Possible Solutions

☑ **7.** List two ways you could combine some of the materials to solve the problem.

_____

_____

Choose One Solution

☑ **8.** Describe your bridge and how you will build it. _____

_____

_____

_____

_____

☑ **9.** List the materials that you will need. _____

_____

☑ **10.** Draw and label a diagram of your bridge.

Designing Bridges

Design and Construct a Prototype

Gather your materials and a ruler. Make two even stacks of three or four textbooks. Place the two stacks 40 cm apart. Build your bridge across the space between the stacks of books. Before you secure your bridge to the books, measure its length, width, and height. Record your measurements to the nearest centimeter (cm).

☑**11.** Record the measurements of your prototype.

Length: _____

Width: _____

Height: _____

Test the Prototype

Test your bridge. First, place a cup halfway across the bridge. Then, place a penny in the cup. Repeat until the bridge breaks.

☑**12.** How many pennies did your bridge successfully support?

Prediction	Testing Results

Designing Bridges

Communicate Results

Add your data to the class data table. Be ready to provide the following information:

Your Name	Type of Bridge	Dimensions of Bridge			Number of Pennies Supported by Bridge
		Length (cm)	Width (cm)	Height (cm)	

Evaluate and Redesign

☑ **13.** Explain how you would change your design to make your bridge stronger.

_____

_____

_____

_____

_____

_____

_____

Designing Bridges

Name _____ Date _____

Career Spotlight Structural Engineer

Can a bridge be blown down in a summer storm? Structural engineers make sure it cannot.

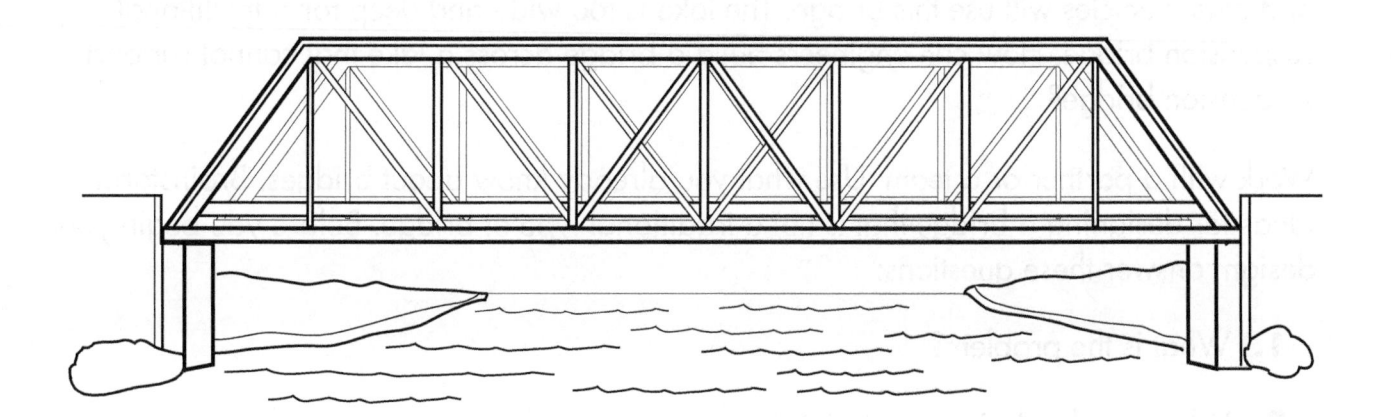

Structural engineers design bridges. They need to know how different forces act on bridges. They need to be sure those forces are safely managed so that the bridges are safe in any weather and under all kinds of stress.

A bridge is affected by the force of gravity. It is affected by the forces of vehicles and people traveling across it. It is also affected by the forces of weather, including wind, rain, and ice. A bridge's towers are affected by the force of waves and the force of water pressure. Structural engineers need to know how to balance all these forces so that bridges are safe.

Designing Bridges

Check Your Understanding

Design It

Two cities on opposite sides of a lake want to build a bridge to connect them. Many cars and other vehicles will use this bridge. The lake is too wide and deep for a traditional suspension bridge. How can engineers build a bridge across a lake that cannot support a suspension bridge?

Work with a partner or a team. Use what you already know about bridges. Brainstorm ideas for designing a bridge that is not a traditional type of bridge. Before you begin your design, answer these questions:

1. What is the problem?

2. What are the design constraints?

3. What environmental factors do you need to consider?

Now, draw your bridge showing all the designs and supports.

Designing Bridges

Enrichment What Are Newton's Three Laws of Motion?

In 1686 Isaac Newton published his book *Principia*. In this book he related forces to the motion of objects. Newton's book put the ideas of many scientists together in a way that people could understand them. He wrote three laws that describe motion.

First Law of Motion	Second Law of Motion	Third Law of Motion
A resting object remains at rest, and an object in motion remains at constant speed and in a straight line, unless acted on by an unbalanced force.	The acceleration of an object depends on the mass of the object and the size of the net force applied.	When a force is applied to an object, the object exerts an equal force in the opposite direction.
Example When you swing a bat, it is at rest until you apply a force to the bat.	**Example** A heavy bat takes more force to move it than a lighter bat takes.	**Example** When the bat hits the ball, the ball flies in the opposite direction. The ball also pushes against the bat. You can feel this force in your hands when you hit the ball.

1. What does the first law say about a moving object if the forces on the object are balanced?

_____

_____

2. Which is greater, the force of the bat on the ball or the force of the ball on the bat? Explain.

_____

_____

Name _____ Date _____

Assessment Designing Bridges

Use the word bank below to complete the sentences.

suspension bridge	truss	force
balanced forces	decimeter	centimeters

1. There are 10 _____ in a decimeter.

2. A push or pull is a _____.

3. A ball sitting on the ground not moving is an example of _____.

4. A _____ can be used to support a bridge.

5. A _____ is a unit of length equal to 1/10 of a meter.

6. Cables can be used to help a _____ stay up.

7. Max and Jaime are on a seesaw. Max weighs 45 kilograms. Jaime weighs 37 kilograms. What could they do to balance out the forces and balance the seesaw?

_____

_____

_____

_____

8. Tyson measures his bridge, and he reports a length of 5 decimeters. Samantha measures her bridge, and she reports a length of 45 centimeters. Who has the longer bridge? Explain your reasoning.

_____

_____

_____

How do you design a strong bridge?

9. A summer camp manager needs you to design bridges to cross over the many streams on their property. The bridges will only be used by people walking. Explain what type of bridge you would use. Draw your bridge.

_____

_____

_____

Designing Bridges

Performance Assessment Portable Bridges

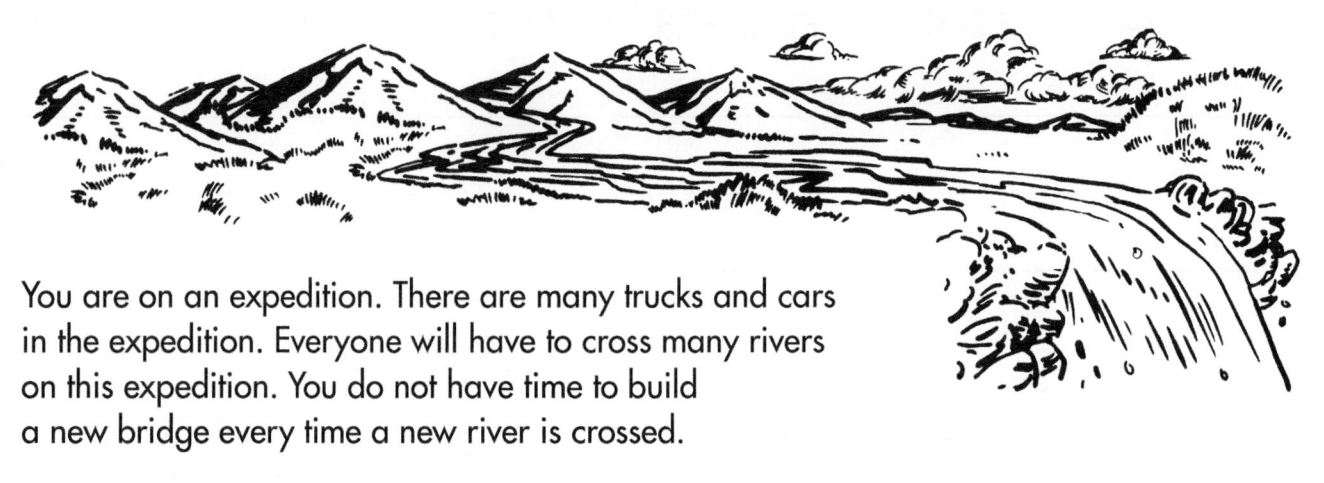

You are on an expedition. There are many trucks and cars in the expedition. Everyone will have to cross many rivers on this expedition. You do not have time to build a new bridge every time a new river is crossed.

You need to design a portable bridge that can be used many times. You can use any type of material to make the bridge, and you can move it any way you wish.

Design It

1. What type of challenges will making the bridge portable present?

_____

_____

2. Design a portable bridge design and describe your design below. Draw your bridge on the next page. Show how it will be made portable.

_____

_____

_____

3. Test your portable bridge. What changes will make it work better?

_____

_____

_____

16B
Designing Bridges

Notes Grid

Designing Bridges

Name _____ Date _____

Standardized Test Prep

Circle the letter of the best answer.

1. Which type of bridge is made of a horizontal beam supported by piers?

   A Arch bridge

   B Suspension bridge

   C Beam bridge

   D Pier bridge

2. Which of these tools would you use to measure the length of a bridge prototype?

   A Graduated cylinder

   B Ruler

   C Balance

   D Thermometer

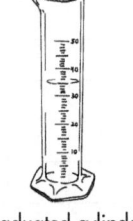
Graduated cylinder

Ruler

Balance

Thermometer

3. A student is told to build a bridge that can span a distance of 80 decimeters? How many centimeters is this?

   A 800 centimeters

   B 8 centimeters

   C 80 centimeters

   D 0.8 centimeters

Designing Bridges

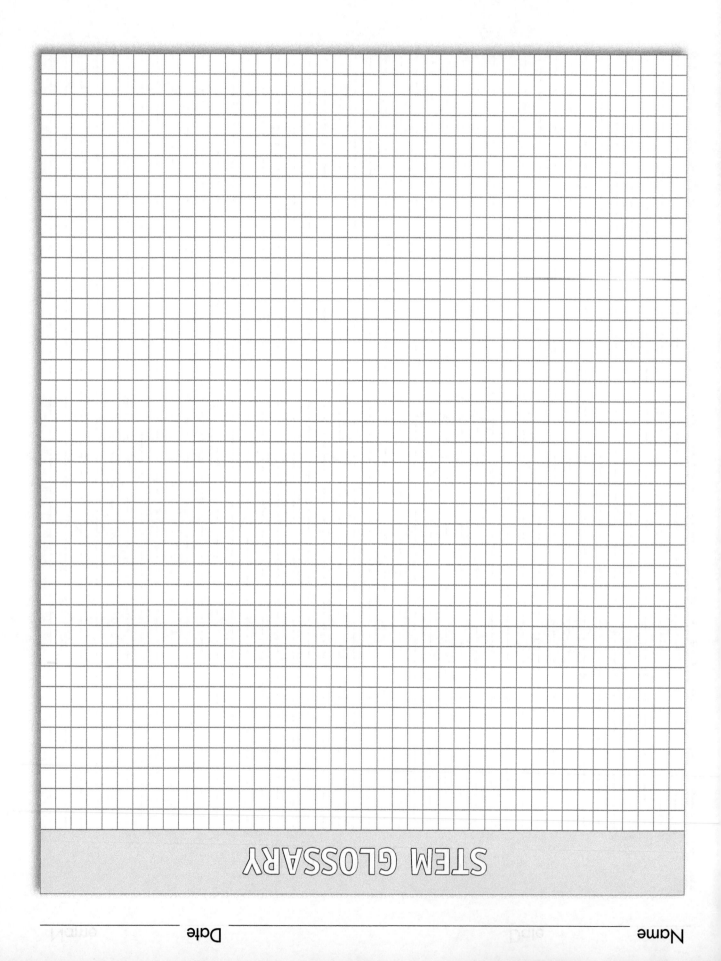